Scary Creatures

DEEP

Written by
Jim Pipe

BOOK HOUSE

Created and designed
by David Salariya

Author:

Jim Pipe studied Ancient & Modern History at Oxford University then spent 10 years in publishing before becoming a full-time writer. He has written numerous non-fiction books for children, many on history and natural history. He lives in Dublin with his lovely wife Melissa and his twin boys, Daniel and Ewan.

Artists:
Mark Bergin
Carolyn Scrace
John Francis
Rob Walker

Series Creator:

David Salariya was born in Dundee, Scotland. In 1989 he established The Salariya Book Company. He has illustrated a wide range of books and has created many new series for publishers in the UK and overseas. He lives in Brighton with his wife, illustrator Shirley Willis, and their son.

Editor: Tanya Kant

Editorial Assistant:
Rob Walker

Picture Research:
Mark Bergin, Carolyn Franklin

Photo Credits: Deep Sea Photography

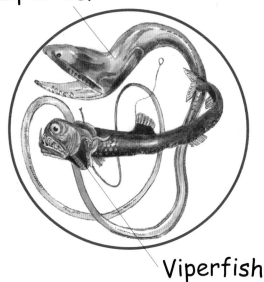

Gulper eel

Viperfish

Published in Great Britain in 2009 by
Book House, an imprint of
The Salariya Book Company Ltd

𝕊𝔸𝕃𝔸ℝ𝕀𝕐𝔸

25 Marlborough Place, Brighton BN1 1UB
A catalogue record for this book is available from the British Library.

HB ISBN: 978-1-906370-89-3
PB ISBN: 978-1-906370-90-9

Printed in China

Visit our website at **www.book-house.co.uk** or go to **www.salariya.com** for *free* electronic versions of:
You Wouldn't Want to be an Egyptian Mummy!
You Wouldn't Want to be a Roman Gladiator!
Avoid Joining Shackleton's Polar Expedition!
Avoid Sailing on a 19th-Century Whaling Ship!

PAPER FROM
SUSTAINABLE
FORESTS

Contents

Deep-sea chimaera

Fishing boat

Trawl net

Giant squid

submarine

Gulper eel

Sperm whale

Did You Know?

The ocean deep is the least explored place on Earth. Just 5 per cent of it has been well mapped. Only two **expeditions** have ever reached the deepest part of the ocean, the Mariana Trench in the Pacific Ocean.

Deep-sea eel

Anglerfish

Light from the sun cannot reach the deepest parts of the sea, so it is always cold and dark. Without light, no plants can grow. Yet even at the greatest depths, 10 km below the surface, the sea is home to all sorts of strange and wonderful animals.

What is the ocean deep?

If all the world's seas were drained away, you would see deep valleys and mountain chains. The tops of some of these mountains peek above the surface as islands. The bottoms of the valleys are the bottoms of the valleys are the ocean deep. This book is about some of the strange animals that live deep in the oceans. If you're brave enough, read on!

Earth's oceans cover more than two thirds of the planet, with an average depth of almost 4 km. The **deep sea** has been in total darkness since there were first seas on Earth, yet it is the planet's largest **habitat.**

Rattail

Sea cucumber

Why are creatures of the deep scary?

In the darkness of the ocean deep, animals need to make sure that when they catch something, it doesn't get away. Many fish have mouths stuffed with razor-sharp teeth. They look terrifying, but most are just a few centimetres across.

Gulper eel

Anglerfish

Snailfish

Viperfish

Did You Know?

The gulper eel has a huge mouth, a long body and a very elastic stomach to help it swallow and store large **prey**. Gulpers can survive for weeks without eating.

Many deep-sea fish will eat animals larger than themselves. Viperfish have hinged jaws that can open incredibly wide.

7

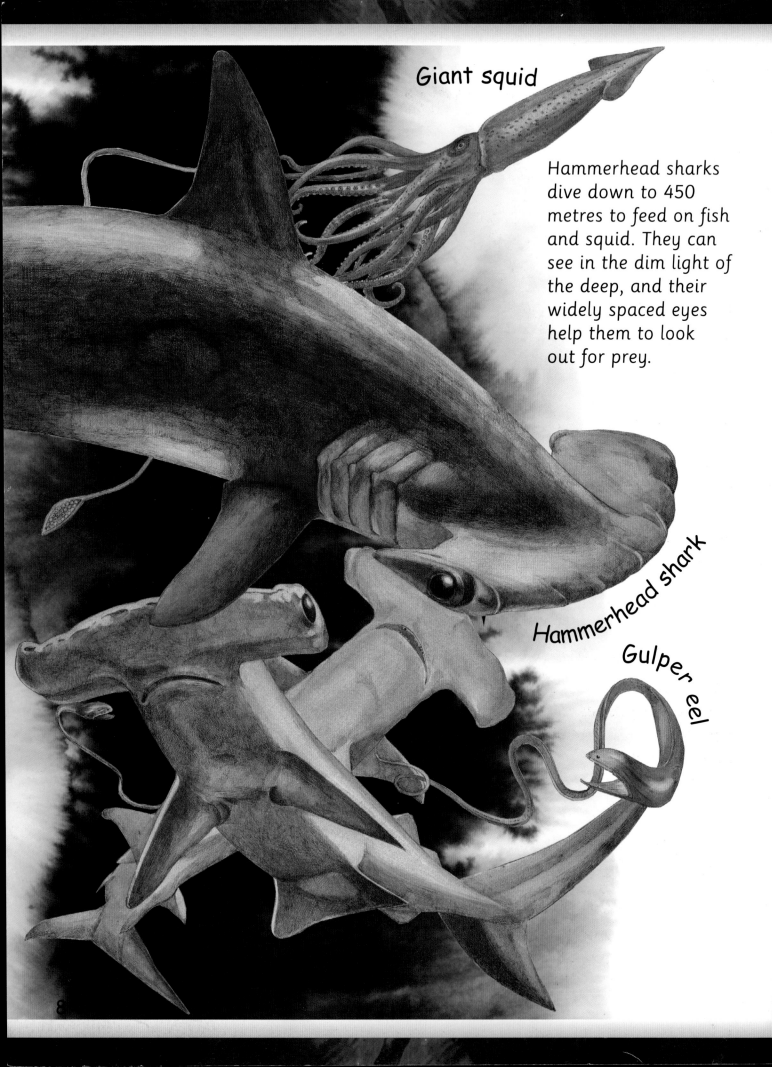

Giant squid

Hammerhead sharks dive down to 450 metres to feed on fish and squid. They can see in the dim light of the deep, and their widely spaced eyes help them to look out for prey.

Hammerhead shark

Gulper eel

8

Why is the deep so dark?

Most sea animals live near the sea's surface where there is plenty of sunlight. Further down there is still some light during the day, but the sun's rays cannot reach below about 1,000 metres. So the ocean deep is completely dark. It's a scary place. A **predator** can attack from above, below or from the sides, and there's nowhere to hide!

What is the twilight zone?

The layer of the ocean from 150 to 1,000 metres below the surface is often called the **twilight zone**. Here there is some sunlight, but lower down the waters are dark. Many of the animals living in the twilight zone, such as luminous prawns, can produce their own light. This helps them blend in with the brighter waters above.

Is the deep totally dark?

Below 1,000 metres, the only light in the water is the sudden flashes made by animals themselves. Though they are no brighter than moonlight, these flashes seem very bright in the pitch-black ocean depths.

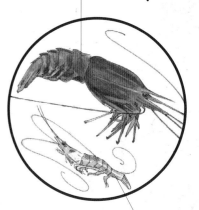

Luminous prawn

Deep-sea shrimp

Did You Know?

The barreleye fish has two big eyes for picking up as much light as possible in the dark deep-sea waters.

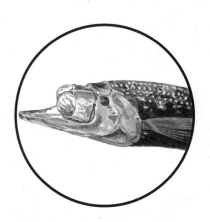

Barreleye fish

Do deep-sea creatures ever swim to the surface?

Some do! They swim up at night to feed at the surface, where there is plenty of food. During the day, they live in the dark depths to avoid predators that would easily catch them in the sunlit surface waters. Some shrimps travel over 1,000 metres up and down each day. They are very sensitive to light, so they stay far below the surface during the day.

Lantern fish

Every night, the lantern fish makes a 2-hour journey to within 100 metres of the surface to look for food. Every morning it takes another 2 hours to swim down again.

Giant squid

The rare oarfish has a snake-like body up to 10 metres long. It needs lots of food, so it probably lives within 300 metres of the surface.

Oarfish

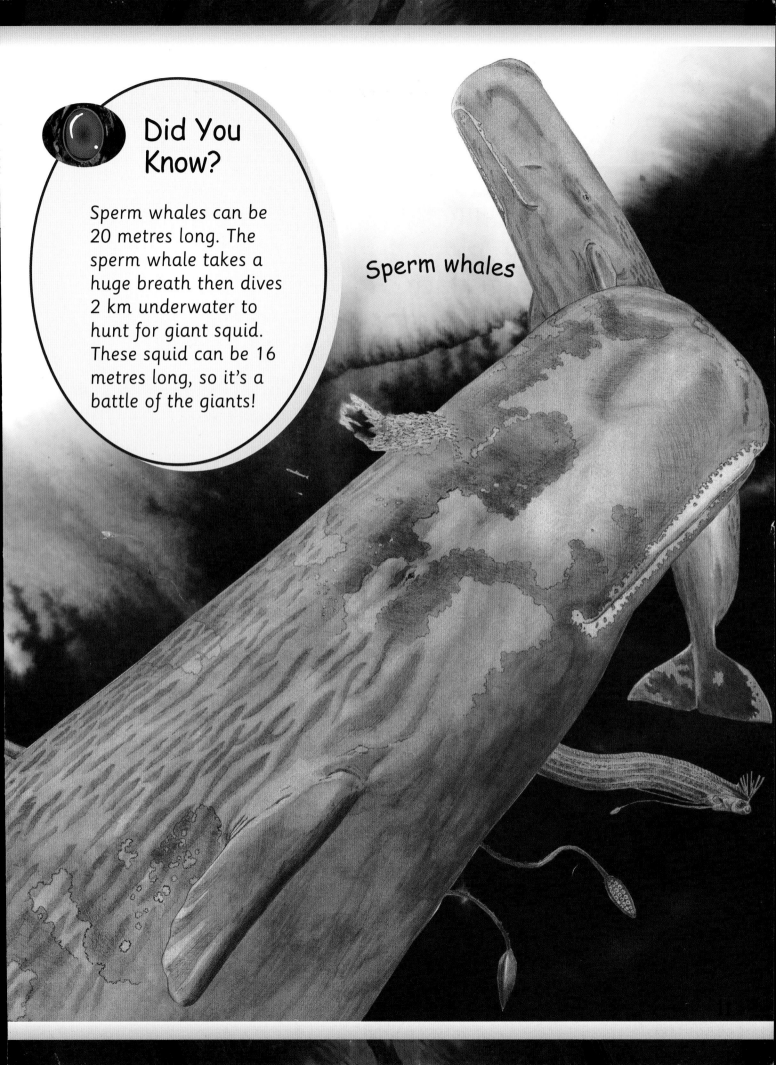

Did You Know?

Sperm whales can be 20 metres long. The sperm whale takes a huge breath then dives 2 km underwater to hunt for giant squid. These squid can be 16 metres long, so it's a battle of the giants!

Sperm whales

Who lives at the bottom?

Slow-moving animals such as sea cucumbers, starfish and sea anemones live on the sea floor. They sit and wait for food to drop near to them. Most food for deep-sea creatures comes from the surface. How does it reach the animals 10 km below? It sinks. When a whale dies, its body drops to the bottom.

Sea cucumbers live in the thick grey ooze that covers the ocean floor. They breathe through their bottoms and spew out their guts to scare off predators!

X-Ray Vision

Hold the next page up to the light and see what happens to the whale's body.

See what's inside

Brittle stars, worms and limpets carpet the **sea bed**.

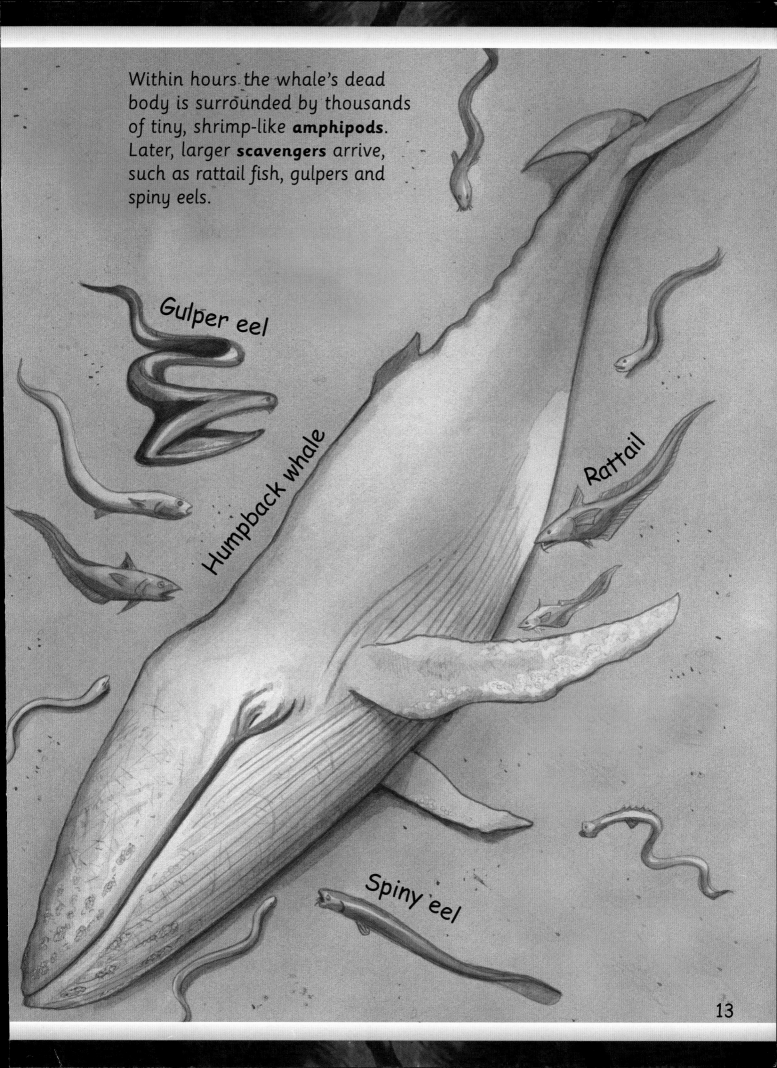

Within hours the whale's dead body is surrounded by thousands of tiny, shrimp-like **amphipods**. Later, larger **scavengers** arrive, such as rattail fish, gulpers and spiny eels.

Gulper eel

Humpback whale

Rattail

Spiny eel

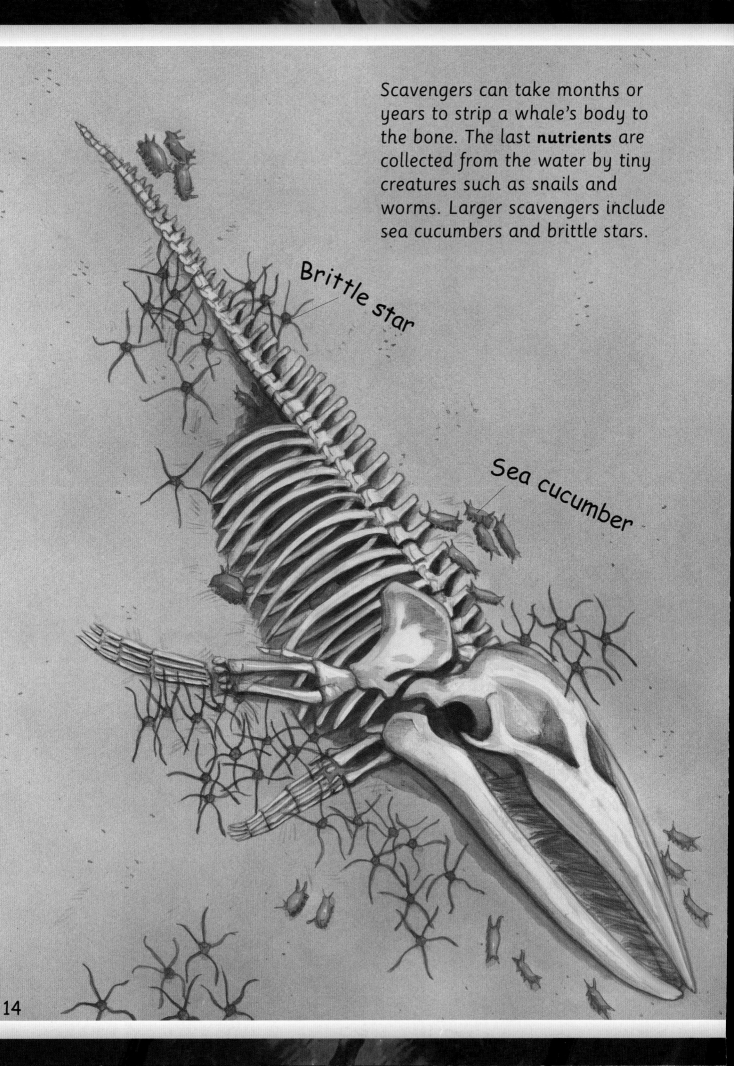

Scavengers can take months or years to strip a whale's body to the bone. The last **nutrients** are collected from the water by tiny creatures such as snails and worms. Larger scavengers include sea cucumbers and brittle stars.

Brittle star

Sea cucumber

Why do some animals have jelly bodies?

In the deep ocean, animals are surrounded on all sides by water. There is no need for a skeleton because the water supports the weight of their bodies. So jelly-bodied animals such as jellyfish and comb jellies are common.

Siphonophore

When it bumps into something, the jelly-like siphonophore glows with a bright blue light. Giant siphonophores are up to 30 metres long – that's longer than a blue whale.

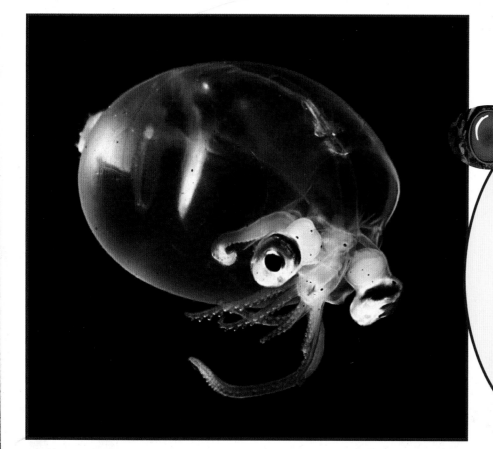

Deep-sea glass squid

Did You Know?

Soft bodies are tempting to predators. Animals like the glass squid have almost transparent (see-through) bodies, so predators will look straight through them!

What sea creatures use jets to get around?

While fish swim using their tails and fins, squids swim using jet power. They suck water in through their mouth, then shoot it out through a tube called a **siphon**. They can move in different directions by changing the direction of the siphon.

The sea angel hunts sea snails using a tongue studded with small, sharp teeth. Its mouth is at the top of its head.

Mouth

Vampire squid

Webbed skin

Eye

Sea angel

The vampire squid looks scary because of its big eyes and red colour. Its name comes from the webbed skin between its arms that looks like the skin covering a bat's wing.

There are many other strange-looking squids in the deep sea. The piglet squid has a pig-like snout and holds its **tentacles** over its head. The cockatoo squid also has tentacles on its head, which look like a tuft of feathers.

Tentacles

Piglet squid

Did You Know?

The vampire squid resembles both an octopus and a squid – it has ten arms, not eight like an octopus. It hangs in the water by drooping its arms in an umbrella shape.

Dumbo octopus

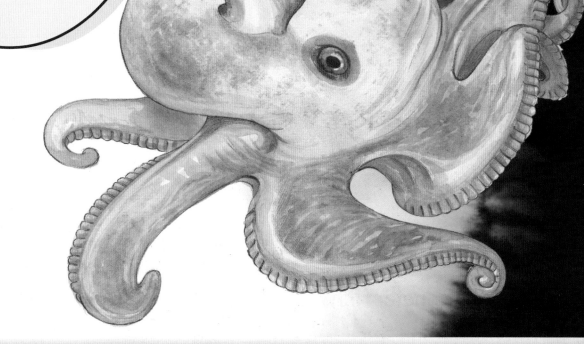

Dumbo octopuses have two fins that look a bit like elephant ears.

Why do deep-sea fish look so strange?

Deep-sea fish look strange to us because they are built for life in the depths. Anglerfish and fangtooths have giant heads for catching prey. Other fish are long and thin, so that they can cut through the water without using too much energy.

Deep-sea chimaera
This strange fish uses its long snout to scan the sea floor. It can sense prey buried in the mud.

Deep-sea anglerfish

Fangtooth or ogrefish

Why do sea creatures glow?

On land, a few creatures such as fireflies and glowworms can make their own light. But in the deep sea, 90 per cent of **species**, from tiny **bacteria** to fish and squid, can make light. This is called **bioluminescence**. Some fish use flashes of light to confuse predators, while others use light to attract prey or a mate.

X-Ray Vision

Hold the next page up to the light and see what glows in the ocean deep.

See what's inside

How do they do it?

Sea creatures create light with special chemicals in their bodies. Most produce a blue light, but some produce green or yellow. A few even produce red light.

What fish goes fishing?

The dragonfish has light organs along the sides of its body, either to attract a mate or to lure fish from deep below. Like the anglerfish, it also has a light at the end of a 'fishing rod' on its chin, which flashes on and off to lure prey. When a fish gets close enough, the dragonfish snaps it up in its powerful jaws.

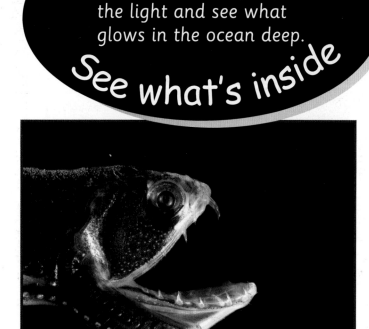

Scaly dragonfish

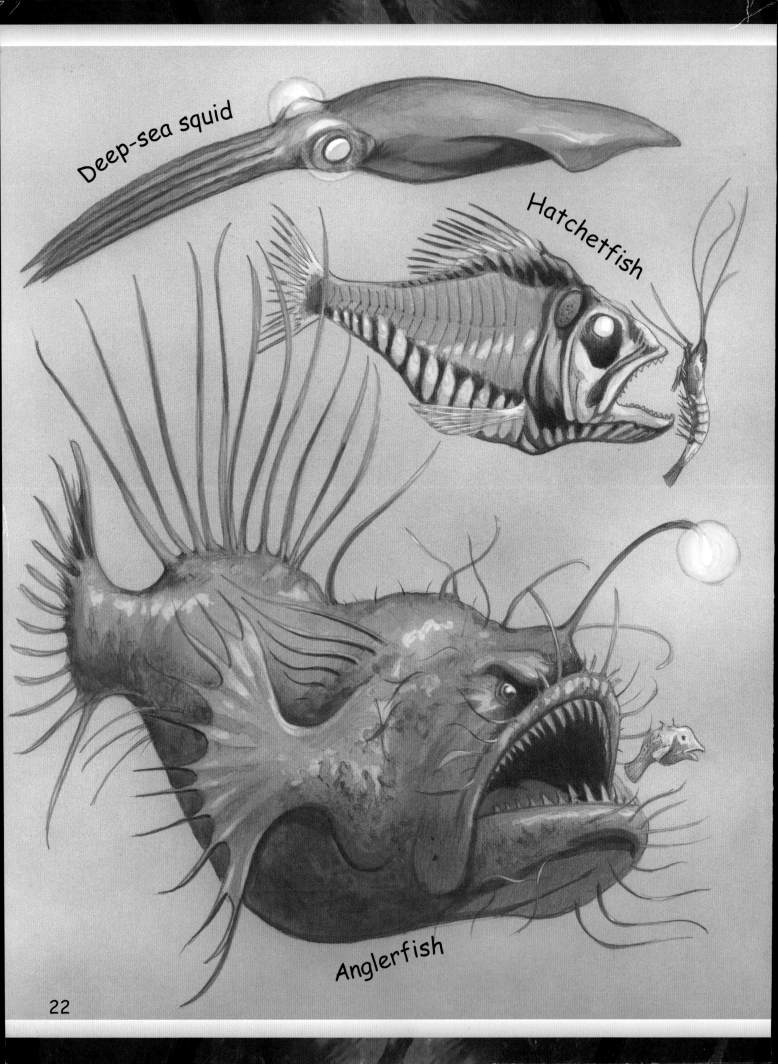

Deep-sea squid

Hatchetfish

Anglerfish

Are there really sea monsters?

No, sea monsters don't exist, despite old sailors' tales of giant, man-eating sea creatures like the Kraken pictured below. In fact, most deep-sea animals are small. The fish that live in the greatest depths, snailfish, are rarely longer than 35 cm.

Did You Know?

The Greenland shark is 7 metres long and has been seen at depths of 2,200 metres. It also comes to the surface to catch prey. An entire reindeer (without the antlers) was once found in a Greenland shark's stomach!

The closest thing to a real sea monster is probably the giant squid. A giant squid couldn't sink a ship, but it's a fast swimmer that uses its long tentacles to grab onto prey. It has powerful jaws like a parrot's beak and eyes the size of dinner plates.

Mythical Kraken

Anglerfish are scary but small!

What smokes at the bottom of the ocean?

Most of the water at the bottom of the sea is a chilly 2–3°C. But in the 1970s, scientists got a shock when they discovered springs of hot water, up to 400°C, gushing up from the seabed. These **vents**, called 'black smokers', look like tall chimneys and release murky clouds of chemicals.

Black smokers can support whole deep-sea communities. The chemicals from smokers would poison most animals, but tiny bacteria use them to make food. Shrimp-like amphipods feed on the bacteria, and bigger animals such as huge clams and giant spider crabs then eat the amphipods.

Giant tubeworms

Scaleworm

Tubeworms are almost 2 metres long and are as thick as your wrist. They grow in clusters near the vents. They have no mouth or stomach, but get nutrients from bacteria that live inside their bodies.

Hot-water vent

Giant tubeworms

Small scaleworms live among the giant tubeworms near the tips of smokers.

Rattail

Did You Know?

Other strange animals found near undersea vents include snipe eels with bird-like beaks and vent shrimp. Instead of eyes, vent shrimp have a pair of organs on their back that detect heat.

Snipe eel

Sea cucumbers

How do you explore the ocean deep?

Some of the most amazing discoveries of the last 100 years have taken place in the ocean's depths. Scientists find new species by using huge nets that 'fly' through the water, 5 km below the surface. They also lower video cameras and electronic sensors from ships to gather information. Mini-submarines and unmanned robots can carry cameras and other equipment to the sea floor.

How deep have we gone?

In 1960, Jacques Piccard and Don Walsh reached the deepest point in the ocean, the Mariana Trench. It took five hours for their **bathyscaphe**, the *Trieste*, to sink almost 11 km. They forgot to take a camera!

Bathyscaphe

Jason Jr

A robot **submersible** called *Jason* can dive to 6,500 metres to take photographs and collect small animals from the sea bed. A similar submersible, *Jason Jr*, was used to explore the wreck of the famous ocean liner, the *Titanic*.

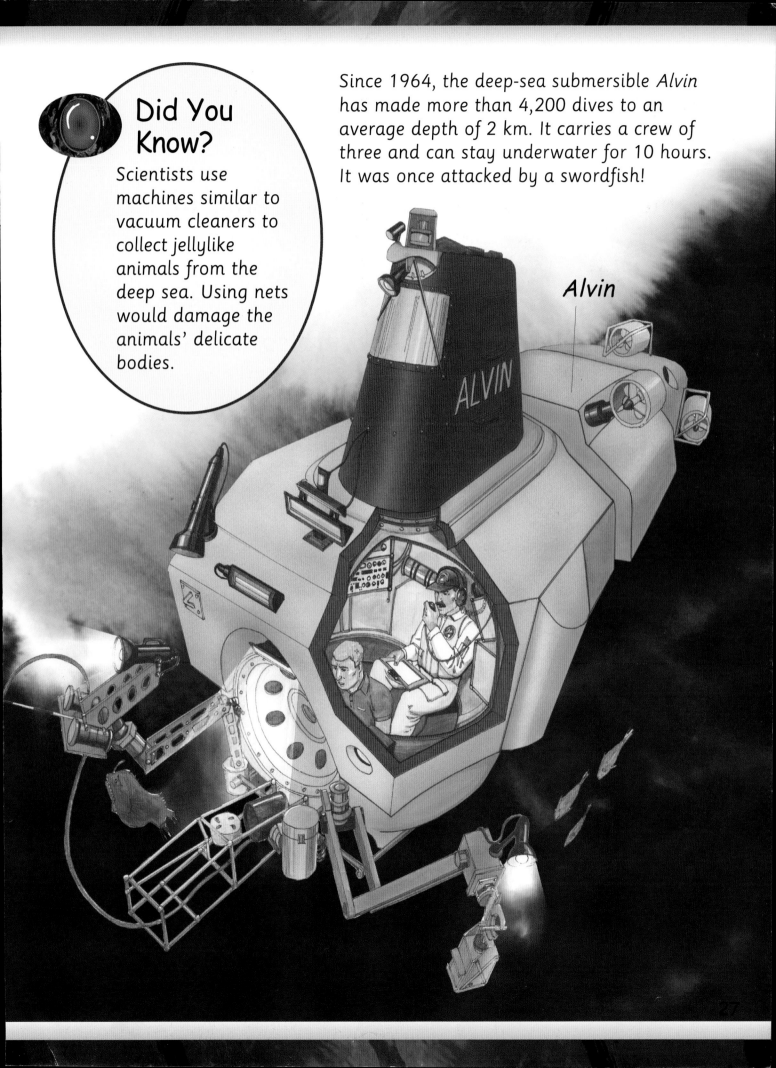

Did You Know?

Scientists use machines similar to vacuum cleaners to collect jellylike animals from the deep sea. Using nets would damage the animals' delicate bodies.

Since 1964, the deep-sea submersible *Alvin* has made more than 4,200 dives to an average depth of 2 km. It carries a crew of three and can stay underwater for 10 hours. It was once attacked by a swordfish!

Alvin

ALVIN

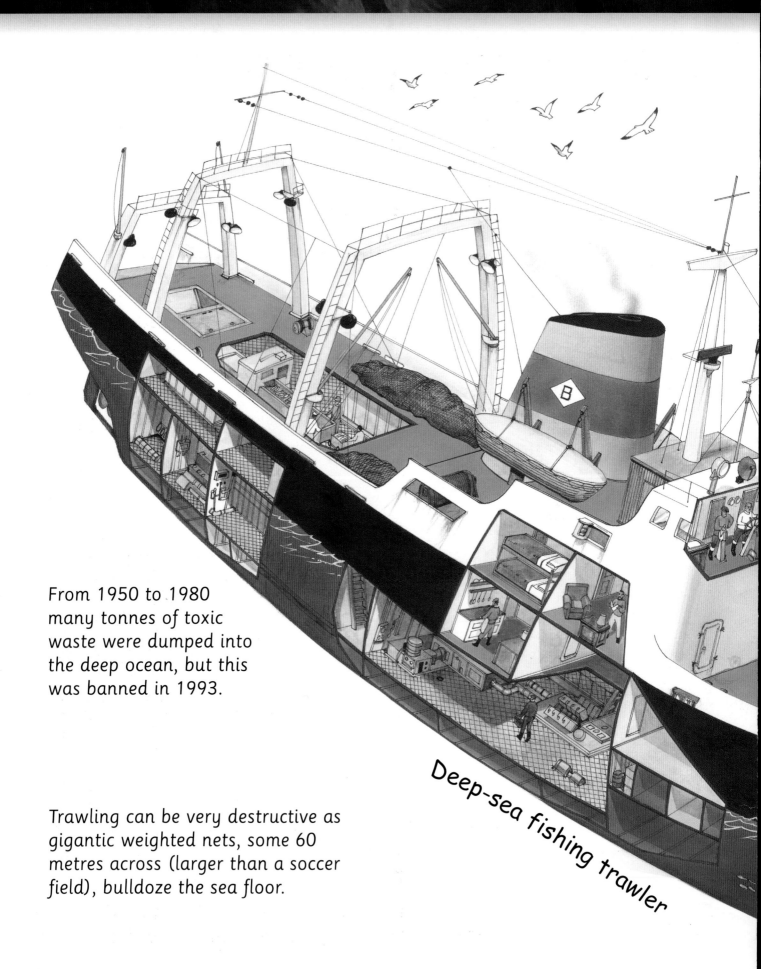

From 1950 to 1980 many tonnes of toxic waste were dumped into the deep ocean, but this was banned in 1993.

Trawling can be very destructive as gigantic weighted nets, some 60 metres across (larger than a soccer field), bulldoze the sea floor.

Deep-sea fishing trawler

Why should we preserve the deep-sea habitat?

We know now that the deep sea is full of life, so it's important that we protect this habitat. Nowadays, fishing fleets use huge trawl nets to catch fish at very great depths. **Trawling** has already destroyed half of the deep-water coral off Norway. The deep-sea habitat is also threatened by companies searching for valuable ores, minerals and oil under the sea bed.

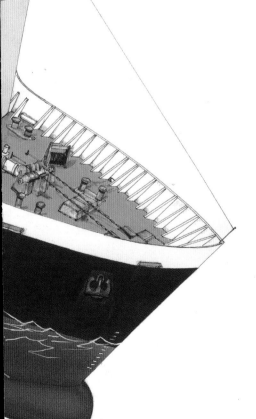

Trawl net

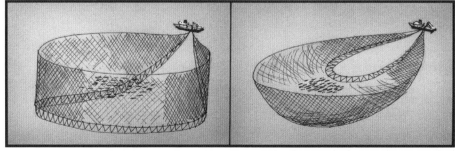

Purse seine

Modern fishing boats use specially shaped nets (shown above) that can catch thousands of fish at a time.

Deep-sea facts

Because they are deep as well as wide, oceans make up 99 per cent of the space where animals can live on Earth. 85 per cent of this is the deep sea, the biggest habitat on our planet.

On average, a new deep-sea species is found every two weeks. Scientists believe there may be millions more waiting to be discovered.

At 150 metres, 99 per cent of the light from the sun has been blocked by the water above. Below 1,000 metres, it is pitch black.

The deeper you go in the sea, the more pressure, or squeezing force, there is. Around 10,000 metres below the surface, the pressure is a thousand times what it is at the surface. But because the bodies of most sea creatures are made up mostly of water, they do not feel this pressure.

The temperature at the bottom of the ocean is a brain-numbing 2–3°C. The water from deep sea vents is a roasting 400°C. However, just one metre away from the vent opening the temperature drops to 5°C.

The gigantic chimneys of black smokers can grow up to 60 metres tall. These are formed from minerals dissolved in the hot water. One 40-metre chimney in the Pacific Ocean was known as Godzilla before it toppled over.

The Japanese robot submersible *Kaiko* could dive 10,000 metres deep, but it was lost at sea in 2003. The manned French submersible *Nautile* can reach depths of 6,000 metres.

The deepest-living fish is a type of snailfish. One was caught at a depth of 7,230 metres in the Pacific.

The heaviest creature in the deep is the sperm whale, which weighs 14 tonnes. The longest is the giant siphonophore. It can grow up to 40 metres long. Though it looks like one animal, the giant siphonophore is actually a colony of many animals, all working together.

Perhaps the strangest deep-sea creature is the jewel squid. Its body looks like a giant strawberry. It has one big eye that looks upwards at sunlit areas, while a smaller eye looks down into the inky darkness below.

In 2005, a crab with hairy legs, nicknamed the 'Yeti Crab', was found by *Alvin* near deep-sea vents in the Pacific Ocean off Easter Island.

Glossary

amphipod A member of a group of crustaceans that includes shrimp, sea lice and sand fleas.

bacteria Tiny organisms that usually consist of a single cell.

bathyscaphe A type of deep-sea submersible.

bioluminescence Light produced by animals' bodies, such as the glow from a firefly or an anglerfish.

deep sea The dark, cold bottom layer of the sea, more than 1,000 metres below the surface. It is also known as the abyss.

expedition A journey planned especially for exploration or research.

habitat The natural home of a plant or animal.

nutrient A substance or chemical in food that provides energy or helps animals or plants grow.

ore A type of rock from which metals can be extracted.

predator An animal that hunts other animals for food.

prey An animal that is hunted for food.

scavenger An animal that eats the dead remains and waste of other animals and plants.

sea bed The bottom of the sea, also called the sea floor.

siphon The tube-like part of a squid that squirts water in order to push the squid through the sea.

species A group of animals or plants that look the same, live in the same way, and can mate with each other to produce young.

submersible A small underwater vessel that is launched from a larger ship.

tentacles Long flexible arms (without bones), often with suckers or hooks for feeding.

trawling Catching large numbers of fish using giant nets pulled behind a fishing boat.

twilight zone The middle layer of the sea, from 150 metres below the surface down to 1,000 metres. Also known as the mesopelagic zone.

vents Also known as hydrothermal (hot-water) vents or black smokers. Created by underwater volcanoes, vents spew out clouds of black smoke.

Index

Dumbo octopus